JEFF SENOUR

LIFE LESSONS FROM
7 MILES HIGH

THE VIEW THAT
CAPTURED MY HEART

LIFE LESSONS FROM 7 MILES HIGH
The View that Captured My Heart

Copyright © 2024 **Jeff Senour**

ISBN (Paperback): 978-1-964494-59-3
ISBN (Ebook): 978-1-964494-60-9

Printed in the United States of America.

PROMINENT
BOOKS
EDGE

5830 E 2nd St, Ste 7000 #9983
Casper, WY 82609
USA

CONTENTS

INTRODUCTION

When I was five years old, my dad took me up for my first airplane ride. It's safe to say that dad was an adventure-seeker who loved life and instilled in me to do the same. He loved trying new things, searching new adventures, seeking new frontiers all the while teaching me to live life and enjoy every day to the fullest. I think he got a kick out of living like a kid through me. From the moment we left the confines of Earth in that beautiful Piper Cub, I was hooked. With the side window open and the wind on my face, we soared through the sky at a brisk 60 mph. So many emotions all at once raced through my soul. Fear and excitement all at once gazing down at the world below, it was the ultimate sense of freedom. I felt this must be how a bird must feel.

We had many flying adventures together and by the time I was 9 years old, I actually was able to control the plane in flight. Barely able to see over the dash, it was liberating to feel the machine in my hands, controlling it through the sky. There I was doing something that was a pipe dream to mankind less than a 100 years ago.

Jeff around 4 years old in a Piper Cub his Dad took him flying.

It wasn't until I was older that I would realize what a gift I had been given, not only from my dad but a gift from God. Little did I know that I would spend my life witnessing the world from the lofty view of an airplane and the perspective of this world it would give me.

After spending over 30,000 hours, roughly 3 ½ years in the air, aviation has taught me many things about life. It's made me realize that this journey is not all about the landing but soaring through this beautiful world, experiencing what each day has in store. Usually it's a clear, smooth day but sometimes there's a storm in our path we have to navigate round or an emergency that pops up we have to take care of to avoid a worsening problem. Aviation has taught me about love, kindness, forgiveness, striving for perfection and never accepting the status quo.

My other passion has been music as my mom was a musician and her DNA must have passed on to me. I never would have dreamt that I would stand on numerous stages in my lifetime, singing the music I wrote to inspire others to live their dreams. It's a rewarding feeling and a gift I never take for granted.

It is my desire that everyone who reads this book will be inspired and motivated to live a life of gratitude and joy as well as finding the flame that burns inside of each us and the gifts that we've been given by God, have gratitude for every day on Earth and to leave this world a better place than when we came into it.

There are almost 8 billion people on earth and no two of us are alike. Each one of us has a purpose, a gift, something that makes us unique and who we are. It's our job to find those gifts and do something good with them, make a difference.

In Jeremiah 1–5 God is speaking to Jeremiah and says, "Before I formed you in the womb I knew you, and before you were born, I consecrated you, I appointed you a prophet to the nations."

Before he created the earth, God knew where and when we would be born and what gifts we would have. I believe we are living in some of the most profound times of human history and we were chosen to be here for a reason. It's our assignment to find those gifts and go amongst this world, be the prophet he created us to be and leave this world a better place than before we came into it.

Enjoy.

Jeff by helicopter at corporate event. They wanted a singing Pilot

CHAPTER 1

WEIGHT OF THE WORLD

Aviation is an excellent metaphor for life. Both are about perspective, coping with fear, and expanding in gratitude.

I believe we are put here by God with our own unique gifts. The beauty of his creation is no two of us are alike and we are placed here for a purpose. It's our job to find those gifts and use them for something good, do something productive and be an asset to this world, not a liability. Since I was a young boy Flying airplanes and playing music was in my blood and I have been extremely blessed to do both. As an aerial film pilot, there are moments of excitement and awe and also on very rare occasion moments where I have had to face fear and the unknown. It's what you do during such times that reveals what you're made of. Filming large aircraft going over 300 miles per hour is as safe as we make it as a result of thorough briefings and protocols. However, there are times unforeseen situations can emerge, kind of like life when we are presented with split second decisions that have to be made.

A safe flight starts with your mindset just like any great thing we do in life starts with a good pre-flight. You prepare by being well-rested and at the top of your game, our best shot at sticking that landing at the end of every mission is by being prepared for emergencies, knowing our contingency plans, and setting ourselves up for success. The best kind of landing anyone could ask for is a safe one of course but as aviators we constantly strive to make that landing the best one. It's a never-ending quest to come as close to perfection as we can, even though we don't ever quite achieve that perfection. It's in our blood to set a goal for the perfect flight and is probably why we are sometimes misunderstood as having big egos. It's not so much about ego as it is about mastering something that takes years to accomplish and do well. Just like there is no perfect day or perfect music performance, there is no perfect flight as well but a constant attempt at doing it better each time.

One of the biggest character builders of my aviation career was filming a Boeing 747 for a commercial airline. As a boy, I would have never dreamt that I would be flying formation with large aircraft for major commercials but here I was. Every time you fly an aerial photo chase, there is a considerable amount of pre-flight planning that goes into it. There is also an extensive briefing with the other pilots and crew to ensure the safety of every flight. From start up to shut down, we brief the flight like a choreographed dance so that every safety aspect is discussed to alleviate any surprises in the air. Flying formation next to a 1 million pound of metal lifted in the sky by its massive wings is safe as long as you're in the right place. Get in the wrong place and it can turn into a fatal experience. Life is like that where things don't always go as planned and many times unforeseen events can change our flight path and even change the way we do things.

It was a beautiful morning in Southern California. We were going to film the engineering marvel of a Boeing 747 for a major airline to show off their product for a commercial. Weighing in at close to 1 million pounds, there is so much wake turbulence that is generated from the lift of its wings, it can easily turn a smaller airplane upside down if caught up in it. Looking at it on the ground, it's hard to imagine something that big can fly let alone cross oceans with ease in a few hours. It's my job as an aerial Pilot to capture the beauty of this machine in flight while at the same time keeping everyone concerned safe. If I place our aircraft in the wrong position, the large behemoth can flip a small airplane like our Learjet upside down in an instant and do significant damage to the plane if not cause numerous fatalities. It's the equivalent of almost 15 semi-trucks fully loaded flying at over 300 miles per hour.

As the aerial pilot/aerial coordinator, it is my job to fly the Learjet like a movie dolly around the other aircraft. The key is to do it smoothly for the camera and stay out of the wake of turbulence to avoid an accident. We fly next to, underneath and all around the massive aircraft to create motion on-screen by slowing down or going across their nose and tail for the dramatic footage you see on commercials and movies.

After our 2-hour brief about the upcoming flight both aircraft took off. We start with what is called an "airborne pickup." We do a flight of two and check in with the tower to let them know both flights are ready for take-off. I took off first and entered a tight traffic pattern while the subject airplane (in this case, the 747) was on the runway, ready for take-off. As I come around from 1,500 feet and make my rectangular pattern, I tell the other pilot to power up in 20 seconds. As I arch around and descend toward the ground at 200 knots, I count down over the radio to the other pilots, 5,4,3,2, and release the brakes. From a standing start, they are accelerating while we are doing around 160mph low to the ground down the side of the runway. When the timing on my part is correct, they rotate to take-off and we are established in formation on their wing and climb out side-by-side as a flight of two. There is so much thrust generated by the subject aircraft when we get close to the runway it's like hitting a wall of air that bumps our aircraft.

We proceeded to choreograph the 747 through many shots of the Sierra Nevada mountains and terrain flying out of Los Angeles International Airport as our natural backdrop. One of our favorite shots we had done many times required the other aircraft to fly under us and emerge out the front of our plane. As long as they had visual contact with us, they could stay a safe distance apart. With a two-take sequence—the first being with our camera lens looking backward while the nose of the colossal jet enters the frame. Then, we would rejoin and do the same thing with the camera looking forward as the subject jet enters and then leaves the frame. With the help of editing, this would look both beautiful and seamless.

We were all set to do the first take, and I got in the lead so the 747 Captain could position behind us to start the shot. Once in position, I told him to accelerate forward. We had done hundreds of these shots before, but for some reason, this one felt different. Through the camera monitor, we watched the giant jet slide through; as it disappeared out of the frame, I had an eerie feeling. I couldn't see him because he was right underneath us. Then, I felt our plane lower slightly like a vacuum was sucking us in. There was a moment of silence and anticipation. Suddenly, like a shark fin sticking out of the water, the tail of his airplane passed by our right window. He had miscalculated his distance from us and gotten too close! It was like a giant whale going by us realizing by God's grace we had just missed hitting each other. Once he passed, there was silence in our aircraft as everyone was processing what happened. It was a miracle the huge airplane didn't hit us—which most likely would've been a fatal, mid-air collision.

There are moments in your life when something happens that shows you who you are and what you're made of. At that moment, I had to contain every emotion I had and exhibit courage to my crew that I was concerned but not outwardly show that I was afraid hopefully giving them confidence that we were ok. As the Captain of my aircraft, it was up to me to show composure, leadership, and courage even when I was scared to death deep down. My reaction calmed everyone down (for the most part). We finished the other shots on our shot list and flew back to Los Angeles for a debriefing. I learned a valuable lesson that day: life can dish things out unexpectedly, and we find out by our reaction at the moment if we have what it takes to face it head-on and triumph.

In today's world, our culture seems to want to avoid any bumps in the road. On that day, as scared as I was, I learned never to take that shot again. When faced with adversity in life it's up to us to come up with solutions to remedy the problem. So, I came up with an idea. We would fly over the top of them and reverse print the footage. That way, we still achieved the same results—but safely.

Even though most people think it's all about the landing, pilots know flying is about more than just sticking the landing. It's a beautiful journey from the pre-flight, taxi out to the runway to the take-off, cruise, and of course, then the finale—the landing. It's like life, in that society expects that every day should be smooth flying, but it's not. Life is filled with disappointments, heartbreaks, illness and every other emotion imaginable. Horrible experiences happen. There could be a storm in your path; you have to figure out how to navigate around it safely. There are smooth days and turbulent days as well in life. Life has never been, and never will be, fair. But overcoming the bumpy flights (and days) gives us wisdom and expands our courage, resilience, confidence, and skill. It also teaches us to be grateful for what we have and appreciate the many good days that come our way. Those storms and turbulence make us feel that much more grateful for the beauty of those smooth-sailing, sun-shining, blissful days. Having something meaningful to fuel our journey helps us to navigate the unfairness and hardships with grace, appreciation, and awareness. We cannot control what life throws at us, but we can respond with courage and compassion for ourselves and others.

As a young boy, my dad was a private pilot and flew as a hobby. I remember like it was yesterday when I was five and he put me in a car seat and flew me around in a Piper Cub tail dragger. My dad was an adventure-seeker and loved taking me with him on many of his journeys. From flying to surfing, scuba diving, and motocross racing, Dad taught me a lot about life and how to live each day with joy and happiness. He taught me to embrace fear and step out of your comfort zone on occasion to test your will. Every year when the air show came to town, we went. We lived in Sunnyvale, CA, near Moffett Naval Air Station. Each year the Blue Angels would come and perform for the masses. The Blue Angels were my favorite. I marveled at the skill it took to fly six fighter jets in synchronization while doing aerobatics close to the ground.

Every time I watched them fly I would be as mesmerized as the year before. As I would marvel at the skill it took to fly like they did, it inspired me to want to become a fighter pilot. Years later, when I was in college, I decided to visit the Air Force and Navy recruiters. There are times in life a dream can be squashed before it's even started because of circumstances beyond our control. As I talked to the recruiter it became clear fairly quickly that perfect vision was a requirement for pilot training. I wore contact lenses for near-sightedness. I was disqualified from a shot at being a fighter pilot before I even had the chance. That moment taught me that those storms in our paths can stop us or lead us to rise even higher and achieve even more. I was determined not to let it stop me and some how some way I would fly airplanes.

In college, I met a person in math class, Royce Jones, who happened to be a flight instructor, and we became good friends. We would talk about aviation and how amazing it is to be at the controls of an airplane. I told him I would love to learn to fly but didn't have a lot of money as a poor college student. One day he offered to instruct me for free if I paid for the airplane. A Cessna 150 was $10 per hour—which was expensive at the time, let alone for a starving college student. I worked every job I could find to barely get by and save enough money to afford a lesson every couple of weeks. I worked fast food, construction, janitorial services, limo driver, printed circuit board inspector, real estate signs, you name it I probably did it. I was invested in learning to fly, regardless of how far away that future felt. Those jobs did teach me about hard work though, all for a common goal of trying to build my hours to become a professional pilot. I eventually got my ratings and did flight instruction for several years to build hours. I also worked in the insurance business. I didn't like insurance but worked for a major insurance company as a marketing rep to fund my dream. I would arrange my schedule to finish my corporate job by early afternoon and take flight instruction into the evening then later became a Flight Instructor. I met so many great people and enjoyed the journey each day all the while building my hours towards my ultimate dream.

I eventually realized that I would have to expand my training and get a Learjet rating if I wanted to advance my career. A friend of mine, Steve Purwin worked at a Lear charter service based at the airport. I admired his life flying movie stars and celebrities around the country to exotic locations. I started to save and save every dime I could so I could obtain my Learjet type rating. It was a steep $5,000 investment at the time, but I knew it would return that investment beyond measure. Learning to fly the Learjet was like going from a Volkswagen to a Formula One racer. It climbed so fast it was hard at first to keep up with it. Jets fly at over 6 miles per minute and can rise 6–8,000 feet per minute. It was such a thrill then and still is to this day. I was like a fighter jet. Bill Lear actually designed the original Lear as a fighter and it was an awesome machine.

The Learjet rating would eventually open some huge doors and I was hired eventually and learned from the best, Mr. Clay Lacy. I went on numerous film jobs with Clay and marveled at his skill in filming aircraft in flight.

Having mentors in our lives are those who help along the way to achieve our goals and Clay became one of mine. He was a United Airlines Captain, air race pilot, aerobatic pilot and aerial film pilot.

He was a celebrity in his own right as everyone in the Aviation world knew him. I learned about high profile discerning customers as it opened the door for me to meet celebrities, CEO's and movie producers who helped me get into Screen Actors Guild flying in TV shows and movies. Then I got the break of a lifetime when working on the set of "Fall Guy" as I was approached by a Hollywood legend, 5-time Academy Award winner Bob Nettmann. He informed me he had heard about my work in the business and was designing an air-to-air film system to house in a Learjet to do air-to-air photo missions.

It was such an exciting prospect that I would literally deliver parts for Bob to be machined or anodized then pick them up just to help speed up the process of finishing the camera system. It showed me that a goal worth achieving would take a lot of hard work and dedication.

There I was in the right place at the right time with a skill set of formation flying and film production that producers needed. We ended up flying film missions for Lockheed, McDonnell Douglas, Boeing and others as well as feature films and TV shows. Who would have known all of that would lead me back to my original dream of flying with Military Aircraft? We were contracted by McDonnell Douglas to fly formation with the Blue Angels and film them as they had just started flying the F-18. It was a dream made manifest. Here I was, the same guy who was ineligible to be a fighter pilot now accomplishing what I had always wanted as I sat in the briefing room with the most elite aerobatic team in the world, the Blue Angels. It felt surreal. Life can change in an instant.

Sometimes disappointment or a storm in our way can turn into something even better than we imagined. Sometimes we might not understand the path to get there but dreams can come true and mine did.

We booked the job with McDonnell Douglas as they manufactured the F-18's and wanted to make a film documentary about the Blue Angels and their new modern fighters. I remember like yesterday as I flew my crew in the Learjet up to Le Moore Naval Air Station near Fresno to brief with the Blues. With pride I stood there on the ramp as the team of six Blue Angels buzzed by at high speed over the airport and broke off in pattern to land. I watched them taxi in and will never forget the excitement that overcame me. I was going to fly next to them, coordinate a film shoot with the legends I'd idolized as a boy. As I stood there, I became that young boy at the airshow all over again, watching them with excitement and youthful awe. Tears came to my eyes. After the introductions and hellos, we got down to business and went over the briefing. Sitting there surrounded by a team of pilots who looked like they just walked out of GQ magazine, I thought I wasn't worthy of being there. But I was so thankful. We went through the protocol of close formation and safety procedures and then were ready to fly.

I remember the "Boss" asking the team if they had any concerns with the Learjet flying as a camera ship. The "Boss," as they call him, made it very clear specific protocols could not be deviated from.

We all agreed and took off in formation, flying over the snow-capped Sierras. We also flew over the Golden Gate Bridge with smoke trailing at 1500 feet. It was a once-in-a-lifetime sight to behold. After our first flight, we came together to debrief once again. Every team member gave a unanimous thumbs up.

Thankfully they were impressed with my flying and my team and how safe the mission was! On the next flight, they were excited to go up and do it again. We did 3 flights with them that day and in the end became friends with the pilots sharing a common bond of aerial ballet in the sky and the privilege it was to do what we do.

We went on to film the Blue Angels on two other occasions. McDonnell/Douglas produced a film called *Ladies and Gentlemen, The Blue Angels,* which used all of our footage. It was a documentary that showed the hard work and dedication the Blue Angels had to have to do what they do. The film won several awards. It's hard to describe the honor I feel to have been part of the production. More incredible milestones would come as I flew with the Air Force Thunderbirds and Canadian Snowbirds as their aerial film pilot. There I was, just a regular kid from Southern California who was disqualified from becoming a fighter pilot but ended up flying next to some of the most talented pilots in our military. Who would have thought? Dreams do come true.

I remember sitting in the briefing room with the NASA test Pilots at Edwards Air Force Base. We filmed numerous missions with them like high angle of attack on the F-18, laminar flow, X-29, X-31, Pegasus

Rocket, yes a rocket launched from a B-52 at altitude and we were next to it filming.

I would sit in the briefing room in awe of the fact that there were Astronauts, Scientists and Engineers who were very intelligent and I had the honor of being a part of something very special.

Understanding that my actions have a measurable impact on the world has been one thing that has made a noticeable difference in my life. My thoughts and dreams help to create the reality I want to experience. Dreams do come true but only with belief in oneself and hard work. When I think about how I can help others, how I can make a difference in this world, how I can leave a legacy behind of something good, I realize that, hopefully, I can be a small part of making this world better a better place than when I was put here by God. I still am and will always be that hopeful, starry-eyed boy that I was at the airshow dreaming and creating a future for myself knowing anything is possible if you try.

REFLECTION POINT

It's our job to find our God-given gifts and use them for something good, do something productive and be an asset to this world, not a liability. List some of your God-given gifts and how you can use them to better the world?

*Landing in remote places where there are no roads
or cell service. Helicopter flying is a magic carpet.
This was near Rosevelt Lake in Arizona*

Jeff flying the Wolfe Air Learjet filming the Bombardier Challenger.

CHAPTER 2

MY HOUSE

CALLED TO SERVE (CTS) is more than just the name of my band. It is how I try to live my life, a life filled with a servant's heart, a life of gratitude and a life of forgiveness and love.

God teaches us to be kind and has called all of us to have a servant's heart, to show love through word and deed and to be grateful for the life we have rather than envious of the things we don't have. Every day I try to set a goal. What can I do to help make the world a better place? But how do I do that? Especially in a world that is so focused on "What's in it for me?" That is where the servant's heart comes in. A servant's heart is focused on putting the needs of others around them first and seeking out opportunities to help. I believe that the world would be a better place if we all did this.

I remember when I learned what a Gold Star family was. As my bandmates and I stood on a huge stage at Oakley Headquarters in Southern California, we anxiously awaited the "Gold Star" families to arrive to perform for them. As we stood there, 22 busloads, over 2,000 people mostly women and children arrived and congregated in front of our stage. Who were these people and why were they called Gold Star families? It suddenly hit me that every one of these people had made the ultimate sacrifice. Every one of them had lost a loved one in Military service in some way. Every one of these people would never get to see their loved one again because they made the ultimate sacrifice while serving in the Military defending my freedom. My band had been asked to play for Snowball Express as part of their event to honor military families. At the time the Iraq and Afghanistan wars were going on and so many of our young soldiers were off to fight in a war half way around the world. As I looked from the stage at 2,000 children, women, and men filling the front of the stage area, I realized that each person there had not lost a mother, father, husband, or wife but a lifetime filled with memories they would have shared together.

Some of the children had never known their father or mother because they had died while serving our country before they were born or when they were very young. Daughters who couldn't seek their mothers' advice when they chose a wedding dress. Some had lost their high school sweetheart, the only person they had loved their entire adult life. All of them made the ultimate sacrifice for their country. Who does that, placing others above self and willing to defend to their death to protect others? Our military, fire fighters and police do and that is the true meaning of a servant's heart. It was a huge honor and privilege to be able to share hope, joy, and faith with these brave families. It was powerful to play music for them, listen to their stories, and be of service. Music is one of the many ways I feel called to do that, to follow the path into God's light and live a life full of compassion and understanding.

The power of music is remarkable. Every song ever heard consists of only 12 notes. There are actually numerous references to the number 12 in the Bible and that it is considered a perfect number which makes the power of music so meaningful.

When did my love for music begin? I would venture to say that it is in my DNA. Growing up, I had an artistic family. My grandfather on my dad's side was a painter. My grandmother on my mom's side a pianist. My mom was a violinist. I always loved the sound of orchestra strings, most likely because of my mother.

Mom came to Los Angeles as a little girl when her parents moved from Canada to Hollywood. They arrived in California in search of a better life. My mom, Daisy, played both violin and piano and started acting at around eight years old. While she never became famous, she did play a part in *Sylvia Scarlett* with Cary Grant. I remember the story of her being on-set at the beach. Cary Grant asked my grandmother if he could take my mom for a walk during a break in shooting, to which she replied, "Absolutely not!" We laugh to this day about mom's missed opportunity to walk with Cary Grant on a Hollywood movie set.

When I was around ten, my passion for music began. I wanted to learn to play guitar. My parents invited a guitar teacher to my house to evaluate my potential. I still feel the disappointment of that day when the teacher said that my hands weren't big enough to play guitar well. I told my parents that I didn't care. I was determined to learn.

This is a lesson that I would carry with me. As long as you believe in yourself, it ultimately doesn't matter what anyone else thinks. My faith in myself and my ideas has led me to a worthwhile and beautiful life. It is when you are true to yourself that you start to live.

My music career with CTS has allowed me to perform on stages at the Pentagon, Soulfest in front of 10,000 people, high schools, Pearl Harbor on the USS Missouri, San Diego on the USS Midway, and many more. It's been a gateway to priceless and unique experiences. I have been in bands my whole life but didn't start writing music until later. I joined my church's worship team and got back into the swing of things musically after being away from it for a while. From that encounter, I met a couple of guys who would form *Called to Serve* with me. Since we had a band, we needed songs. I picked up my pen, and I began to write.

I don't know why I didn't start writing music earlier. I found the process rewarding. One of the first songs I ever wrote was based on the poem "Footprints." We all know it; there are two sets of footprints in the sand. Where there was only one set, that was where God was carrying the author. That story inspired me to write one of my first songs.

Jeff on stage at Chandler Performing Arts Center

Once we had written some songs, we began performing in Church venues as a Christian band but really wanted to touch people's lives in a positive way so we played in secular venues. We realized that we wanted to play in other venues in addition to Churches so we could inspire people of all ages to live a purpose-filled life through the message in our music. By making our music about something bigger than ourselves, we started getting bookings at festivals, fundraisers and even schools. Every song I write has a good message about life-bringing kindness, joy, happiness and purpose through our melodies and lyrics. To date, my band and I have had the privilege of performing in front of thousands of people on stages across America, planting a seed of hope in the hearts of the audiences we perform for.

My band, *Called to Serve*, has been a journey of perseverance for me. There will always be people who don't believe in you, even bandmates who might turn on you. I could tell so many stories of bandmates who just didn't have the same vision I felt for the band and several times parted ways. Even when you are on the same page, it's four different personalities and egos with talent trying to make the music and their ideas happen.

One idea of aligning my band with its true mission came to me as I watched my oldest daughter perform for a school orchestra recital. My children also have a love for music, as I do, as my mother did before me. Julia Claire learned the violin in junior high. Now at twenty seven years old, she's still a gifted musician and now a wonderful mother.

One day, as I was watching her on stage doing an orchestra concert and I came up with the idea to embark CTS on a new road. I thought about how fun it would be to have my music scored for orchestra so I could perform with high school bands. My goal was to combine rock with classical music to tour and play concerts helping raise money for music programs as well as inspiring our youth to live their dreams. I saw how the show could inspire students to pursue their dreams and become whatever they desired to be. I went full force with the idea and created the *Freedom Rock Experience*.

Called to Serve would perform with high school orchestras to help them raise money for their music programs and inspire students in a big way. We had our music scored for orchestra and band. We showed them the value of faith, family and country through our music. We inspired the students and emphasized how lucky we are to live in a country like America where we are free and can achieve great things if you are willing to work at it.

We play at high schools all across the country, empowering students and honoring veterans and first responders. It's been a powerful way to bring patriotism back into schools and children's lives from the east coast, west coast, and everywhere in between.

Jeff, Joe McGinnity, Jerry Nuzum and Dylan Elliott
of CTS in front of a corporate jet.

We often meet inspired young people, having the opportunity to mentor them. The show's production demonstrates to the kids that the work involved in performing—practice, rehearsals, line producing, and then playing the actual concert is also rewarding. We would even get them involved in selling tickets to the show so that they had a hand in raising money for their music program.

They felt invested in the process, taking ownership of their destiny. Shy orchestra kids were given a chance to come out of their shells, shine their light and embrace life.

Nothing is quite as rewarding as the day of a concert, 150 kids on stage with my bandmates and the power of songs I was blessed to have written. I get teary-eyed every time I turn around and see all those violins and cellos bows in harmony with the songs I wrote. Knowing what the experience means to the kids and seeing the smiles on their faces is priceless. CTS became a vessel to deliver inspiration to our youth and our audiences of spreading kindness and hope across our lives, to make each day count as the gift life is. God put us here for a brief time to make every moment count and to live fulfilling, happy lives. But so many don't as they trudge through life just hoping for the best or becoming a victim of everything in their minds. It's up to all of us to inspire others to live their dreams and make each day meaningful.

CTS performing at Dream City Church, "We The People"

I could recount so many stories of kids coming up to me after the concert and saying it was the most fun they had ever had in their lives. We've kept in touch with some kids through their college years and beyond. They tell us their experience with CTS taught them never to give up and gave them the courage to live their dreams.

John, a cello player, was one of those students. He was incredibly introverted and shy. I used to get the kids pumped up by telling them they were in a rock concert, and this was their chance to let loose and have some fun. John came up to me after the show, asking if he could speak with me.

He told me that he just wanted to let me know that CTS was the most fun thing he had ever got to do.

Another student, Ashley, lived in a military town called Harker Heights, Texas, near Ft. Hood. We flew in to play with her school orchestra. Most of the kids in that group had one or both parents in the military. Many had lost a parent, meaning they belonged to a Gold Star family. Ashley's parents were divorced, her mom was a kind woman, keeping things together, ensuring that her daughter had a good childhood.

She and her mom flew out to a school in Mesa, AZ, where CTS was playing, and Ashley ended up performing with my daughter JC. They became fast friends. Ashley went on to accomplish a lot, becoming a nurse. To this day, she still says that the *CTS Freedom Rock Experience* was one of the most inspirational things in her lifetime.

There are many stories like Ashley's and John's. It is my dream to perform at schools across America to inspire our Youth to live their dreams.

Once, we played a concert in Amarillo, Texas. Amarillo is a huge military town and is very patriotic. It was a show that combined two schools; Amarillo High and Tascosa High. We got there, and a friend of ours, Admiral Jack Barnes, had arranged for a Patriot Guard escort and a limo to take us to our hotel. We were treated like true rock stars! We even had a motorcycle escort and limo as we were welcomed to Amarillo.

For me, music entails so much more than the material successes of the world. Good singers are a dime a dozen, and good guitar players can be found on every street corner. That doesn't guarantee anything in music. You have to believe in something bigger and more powerful than yourself and channel that. It has to be bigger than you.

I think God has blessed our vision. That is why we have been able to play on stages small and large, from high schools to the USS Midway, to celebrate the 105th birthday of the oldest Pearl Harbor survivor. Recently we had the honor of performing at Soulfest in New Hampshire at the Gunstock Ski Resort. We played in front of 10,000 people for the candlelight service. As I watched one candle light several more and those light more it made me think of the metaphor of how one light in the world can change so many others. As I stood on that stage listening to over 10,000 people singing in unison with us, it gave me such a feeling of pride and honor and the gift God gave us to be there. Our vision through our music has created something that resonates with so many different people. We don't call ourselves a Christian band but rather a band of Christians because our message is one of hope and positivity that the world needs. No matter what belief someone has, it's pretty difficult to dispute a message of kindness, love, forgiveness and compassion for others.

*Jeff with Ray Chavez, oldest Pearl Harbor
Survivor at 104 years old in the picture.*

One of the most amazing things is when people come up to me and tell me how much a song has impacted their lives. To hear songs I wrote, like *Scrapbook* or *Heaven*, helped them get through the death of someone they loved, that's what keeps me going. We can make people sing or laugh or cry through what we do on stage. For a little while, we can help them remember what is really important to them. Music can have a powerful impact, and that's why I feel so blessed to do this.

From being the young boy who was told by a guitar teacher that maybe he should take up another instrument to performing on stages across America, inspiring audiences of all ages to live their dreams. After 20 years of perseverance to have been signed recently to a record label with Universal Music Group, and Mi5 Recordings, I am humbled and honored to have the opportunity and responsibility of touching lives out there in a positive way. Recently we made #13 on the Global Rock Radio Charts and after 10 weeks still going. Who would have thought and it's such an honor to be a part of that accomplishment.

God has given us this gift of life. It is up to you to decide how to make the best of it.

Every opportunity I get to stand on stage and play, no matter if there's five or five thousand people, I love to look them in the eye and think about how each one of them has a story, a journey, a purpose and for that brief moment I get to engage with them while we perform our music. There are almost eight billion of us on planet Earth, and no two of us are alike. What is your gift? What do you do? Do you put your life on autopilot? Or do you control your life? What is that fire in you that ignites you to do something great for others?

You already have what it takes to make a positive difference, to leave the earth a better place than you found it, and inspire the lives of many. Once you recognize what that unique thing is that inspires you to do good in the world, you will find a life full of blessings. It won't always be pain-free or straightforward; life rarely is. Yet, when you lead with compassion and purpose, others will follow in your light.

Jeff and the band on stage in Dallas for Snowball Express.
Over 2,000 Goldstar widows and children honoring our fallen Veterans.

REFLECTION POINT

God teaches us to be kind and has called all of us to have a servant's heart, to show love through word and deed and to be grateful for the life we have rather than envious of the things we don't have.

How can you be a servant over the next 24 hours?

CHAPTER 3

BEST OF TIMES

As a film pilot in blockbuster movies and flying successful people on private jets, it's always an honor to meet them and see the American Dream in action.

Over the years, I've been blessed to have worked on TV shows and Hollywood hit films like *The Fall Guy, Murder She Wrote, Forever Young, True Lies, Space Cowboys, Executive Decision*, and *Hot Shots*. One thing I have realized from working with and meeting all these celebrities is that at the end of the day, they are just human. Being a corporate and film pilot allows you a peek into their everyday lives, where you get to see them as whom they really are, for the most part just regular people.

I've learned that our differences as people are not as profound as they might appear, and the gap can be bridged through understanding and keeping an open mind. I recognized early on that the most famous people on the globe are just regular people. They experience the same ups and downs, feelings of love and heartbreak, health concerns, family issues and even what fashions to wear as we do. They just have a lot more money and fame than many of us but still laugh and cry the same as humans do.

I have been blessed for the opportunities of flying celebrities, movie stars, former Presidents, and CEOs of major companies around the country. Delivering top-rate service to the discerning high-class travelers was what I learned to do well from great mentors and loved doing it let alone make a living at it. I had the honor of flying movie legends like Bob Hope, Tom Cruise, Clint Eastwood, Johnny Carson, Ann Margaret, Jay Leno, Arnold Schwarzenegger, David Hasselhoff, Goldie Hawn, Kurt Russell, Barry Manilow, and Whoopie Goldberg, Christopher Martin, Rob Walton, just to name a few.

One of my fondest memories was flying Kurt Russell and Goldie Hawn to Aspen, Colorado. We used to fly them there fairly regularly as they owned a house there. There are certain airports that garner the respect of every pilot and Aspen is one of them. Nestled in a valley surrounded by 14,000-foot mountains, Aspen is one of the most difficult airports in the country to fly into. I have always enjoyed the challenge of Aspen and flying a jet into that airport. Surrounded by huge mountains on all sides, Aspen is tucked into beauty of the Rocky Mountains. Every corporate Pilot knows the challenge Aspen can be and is respected by all aviators as one of the toughest airports to get in and out of. Kurt Russell and Goldie Hawn were some of the nicest people you'd ever want to know. We were scheduled to fly them into Aspen then stay for several days until it was time to take them home to Los Angeles. Little did I know at the time that several years later I would end up working with Kurt Russell on *Executive Decision*.

When we arrived at Aspen Airport, we were unloading their luggage and Goldie innocently asked, "Oh, Jeff, are you going go skiing while you're here?"

As I thought for a moment not quite knowing how to answer, I responded, "Oh no, we're just going to hang out in Aspen and look forward to flying you home, but thank you. You both have a great time though."

I didn't have the heart to tell her that I couldn't even afford to go skiing and only made $60 a day at the time. Back then, we didn't make much money starting out, building our hours for experience and just happy to have a job flying a jet. It was an era of Aviation where you had to pay your dues to build hours, even do a lot of things that weren't flying related like mopping floors and delivering parts but you just did it because you had the passion and burning desire to fly an airplane for a living. I used to think, and still do to this day, about how the Wright brothers must have felt as they embarked on the miracle of flight having no idea how to fly or even if it would fly. I felt grateful that even though I wasn't making a lot of money, I was making a living at something the Wright brothers would have given anything to experience, the thrill of flying an aircraft at 600 mph at over 7 miles above the Earth.

Jeff with Jerome LeBlanc aka Maverick and Brian Ernst aka Iceman with the book "Life Lessons From 7 Miles High"

I might have missed an opportunity to go skiing with Kurt Russell and Goldie Hawn but just the honor of meeting them and flying them in a machine that just a few years ago was a pipe dream made me feel very privileged. I felt no regrets for not going skiing and at the same time felt joy for them that they earned the right to be enjoying their lives skiing in such a beautiful place as Aspen. Most aviators can relate to the feeling of that passion that exists inside us, that flame that burns in our hearts that we actually get paid to fly a time machine through the sky in the upper atmosphere of this planet. Relatively speaking it's like a family, a brotherhood and sisterhood of a group of people that share a common passion of flight. Aviation takes a high level of concentration and dedication to do well as safety is a paramount goal of what we do.

One of my favorite celebrity flights was when I got to fly Bob Hope and his wife, Dolores. The plan was to fly them from Burbank, California to Orlando, Florida in the Learjet. We were told that our job was to drop them off safely in Orlando and then turn around and fly home empty to Burbank. Flying lesson number one, always pack an overnight bag. Thinking that we would return immediately, I didn't pack any overnight provisions. When we met Bob and Delores at the airport, they were some of the friendliest people you'd ever want to meet. We loaded them up and off we flew to Florida. On the way there I had a chance to chat with both of them and have great conversation. I remember telling him how much we all appreciated his work with the troops performing for the USO events.

In the course of our conversation, he asked where we were staying in Florida because they would be flying back with us the next day. *Uh oh* I thought, *I have no overnight provisions, didn't bring an overnight suitcase or anything.* My thoughts raced, it was Bob Hope one of the great legends of all time, I couldn't tell him we were just dropping him off in Florida.

So, I replied, "I'm not sure where we're staying yet but we will let you know, sir." Aviation just like life at times takes a twist or a turn not just in the air but learning how to deal with people we come in contact with. Bob and Delores Hope were two of the most gracious, humble people you could ever meet and I am humbled that I had the opportunity to get to know them.

As a Southwest pilot, they used to tell us in training that every time we released the brakes of the airplane, there was over a billion dollars of liability at stake if something big went wrong. If you started counting at this moment from 1 to 1 billion in seconds it would take 31 years to count to a billion. That's a big number and a lot of potential things at stake for a job we tend to take for granted sometimes. I've always kept that in the back of my mind when people would tell me they thought the airplane was all automatic... like we sit at the front of the cockpit and push a button and the plane just goes to its destination. Sometimes I will nicely tease the passengers and tell them that the new apps on our phones are amazing and all I have to do is type in our destination airport, say Phoenix and it goes there. I've also joked with them and said that I have watched a lot of YouTube videos about flying. It's always fun to see the look on their faces.

As we exist in a world that everyone seems to be an expert at everything, it's easy to forget that each one of us as people possess different gifts, God-given gifts, something we are good at.

We're not good at everything but great at something. If life was "automatic" then anyone could do anything well. I have always tried to inspire people to find their gifts within and try to do something good in the world with those gifts. If you can make a living by using those gifts then that's even better. I have been blessed to have made a living at two of my God-given gifts, aviation and music and that is something I try to never take for granted.

Jeff with Marine on stage at concert Mesa Performing
Arts Center along with High School orchestra

Another one of my favorite customers was John Travolta. I used to fly him quite often and was one of the nicest people you'd ever want to know. John was a pilot as well as a famous actor and had the same love for aviation as I did. When he purchased his first jet, a Learjet, the insurance company required that a qualified captain go with him until he obtained enough hours on his own to be a captain. I spent many flights and hours with John and enjoyed our conversations. On one occasion, I was on call and got paged, yes back then we had pagers. Whenever we were paged, we would have to pull over to find a payphone. I know that many people today might not have ever seen a phone booth but you would place a quarter in the phone to make a call. When I talked to the dispatcher, they informed that John Travolta wanted to go to Santa Barbara and needed to leave as soon as possible. I informed her that I had my son Matthew with me for the weekend and couldn't leave him alone since he was about 7 years old at the time. The dispatcher said "Hold on," and in a few minutes came back on the line and said that John Travolta had told her that my son could come along with us.

Matthew my son ended up sitting in the back with John Travolta and they talked and had a great time while we flew to Santa Barbara. Matthew wasn't the least bit influenced by the fact he was on a private jet with a famous person. He was just having fun. My son and I, to this day, still talk about that wonderful experience and how nice John Travolta was. One evening while John and I were waiting for his friends to arrive to fly them, we were out on the tarmac at the FBO in Burbank and started a very interesting conversation. As we sat under the beautiful Southern California nighttime sky I will never forget when he said, "Jeff, my hope is that one day I would just like to meet a wonderful woman and get married, settle down and have kids."

I said, "What?" I was in shock.

I said, "You're kidding! You're John Travolta."

He said, "That's the thing when you're famous, it's hard to find someone who is real, sincere, who actually loves you for who you are, not what you are."

He wanted someone that cared for him and who wasn't after his fame. That moment made me realize a lot about stardom: the rich and famous are no different than the rest of us. They want to be accepted and loved for who they are. We tend to forget that.

Celebrities desire things outside the limelight. They have the exact needs in life as we do, the same habits when they're at home by themselves, and yet we seem to put them on these pedestals. That can be a slippery slope; idolizing the rich and famous when they can cry the same tears or laugh at the same things as the rest of us. It can also make us feel more unhappy in our lives, less grateful for what we have.

When we constantly think there is something more promising, we forget to appreciate what is there. It's easy to have envy and not be thankful for what we have. Each day is a gift to be cherished no matter how famous or average we are. In the end it doesn't matter what kind of car we drive; how big our house is or how much money we have in the bank. What matters is how many lives we touched, who we have to love and who loved us back. What matters is how much kindness, love and forgiveness we spread in this world and the lives we touched. I learned you don't have to be famous to accomplish that.

Flying gives perspective in more ways than one.

The hours I've spent at over 40,000 feet, have made me realize what's important in life and that even the world's biggest stars are no different than the rest of us. Love is always the way and always the answer. Serving from the heart applies to everyone, no matter what stage of life they are in. No matter how much money or fame someone has, none of it guarantees happiness. It made me realize it's not the money or fame that brings happiness but what's inside our hearts. Possessing a servant's heart means to do so with purpose and kindness. Where it may lead is a mystery that only the journey can reveal. Likely, the journey alone will be worth it.

One of my fondest memories was when I would fly Clint Eastwood. I used to fly him quite often to Sun Valley, Idaho. I got to work on several of his movies, *Every Which Way but Loose* and *Space Cowboys*. Clint was always kind and he was always down to earth. On every set you would find the same loyal crew on every show he did. One of the many times I took him to Sun Valley, the job involved staying a couple of days and then taking him back to Los Angeles. The other pilot and I wanted to see a movie, so we went to the only theater in town. We saw *Rambo*, and during the entire film, a group of people in the back was carrying on loudly. As tempting as it was to say something, we refrained. When the movie was over, the lights came on. We stood up, and there was Clint Eastwood and his friends!

"Hey, it's you guys. How's it going?" Clint said. I was relieved we hadn't complained!

I knew Jay Leno because I would pick him up in a helicopter at the station at NBC. One day I was driving home from Burbank airport, and there was this great Excalibur car. I admired it as I waited for the light to turn green, and I noticed the driver was Jay Leno. As we sat and waited at the light with our windows down we started conversing.

"Hey! I know you. You've been my Pilot" He said. I said, "Hi, Mr Leno, how's it going?"

"It's going great." He says. "Wow, great car!" I say.

"Thanks, It's an Excaliber" he says.

The light turned green and we said our goodbyes and drove off.

Looking back, I find it a bit funny that I said that. Everyone knows Jay Leno is into cars and I didn't know what else to say. He was such a nice person though and I was humbled he actually remembered me.

I flew Arnold Schwarzenegger and his wife Maria on occasion when I worked on *True Lies* with him. I was always impressed with Arnold. He was gracious, personable, and considerate when it came to his fans. Kids would flock to him for autographs, and he would happily sign them, quickly making conversation with the kids. He knew how to get along with everybody; I really appreciated that about him. Our job on the True Lies set was to film the Harrier Jet strafing the bridge in the Florida Keys with the bad guys on the bridge. The timing of this shot was critical as I was to direct the Harrier Jet to the proper point on the bridge so the charges in the water were lined up. All the while having the truck on the bridge at the precise point where the Harrier and bullet charges would be timed perfectly for a good shot. I told James Cameron that I wanted to rehears it until I got the timing correct. He told me that I could rehearse the sequence all I wanted but when I said I was ready it better work. In the end the shot worked perfectly but it took every bit of skill in flying to make it happen. It was a good lesson to me as I learned to never let any obstacle stand in your way of achieving something.

Tom Cruise, who I also flew several times, was also a nice person. At the time, I even used to own a Pitts S2B plane. Those in the aviation world know it. A biplane, almost like a sports car, powerful and very aerobatic. Now and then, he would rent our plane when his S2B was down for maintenance. Tom checked out and rented our aircraft on numerous occasions and one day in particular an interesting thing happened while he was taking a friend up. As they taxied out, they forgot to lock the canopy. It's an easy thing to forget if you get distracted.

So, as Tom took off and pushed the power-up in the Pitts, the canopy was unlatched. When the plane was at full power the airflow from the prop blew it right off the back of the airplane. He felt pretty bad for what had happened and wanted to make it up to my partners and I for the damage it caused. He not only had a brand-new canopy installed on the plane but also paid for a top-of-the-line Bose Intercom system to be installed in our airplane. He gave us the Bose intercom system (as a token of his regret, to show how sorry he felt.) It was an honest mistake, and yet he had the heart to do that.

I went on to fly for several companies over the next few years and eventually became a chief pilot for a charter company out of Burbank. I met many interesting successful people including many in Hollywood that everyone knew. I found that good service and kindness went a long way in opening up many doors for my future. I met several movie producers through flying and was eventually asked to work on several shows. I was hired as a pilot for several TV shows and was able to join the Screen Actors Guild.

One day I met a gentleman by the name of Bob Nettmann while shooting a commercial. Bob was an interesting individual as he was a 5-time Academy Award winner for his designs in film systems.

He had invented gyro stabilized camera mounts for helicopters and such. At the time he was inventing a system called Vectorvision which he wanted to design as an improvement to a previous system called Astrovision. Astrovision was a periscope camera system housed in a Learjet that created a God's-eye view in flight of another aircraft. The Learjet was used as a 300mph dolly to take motion pictures of aircraft in flight. Vectorvision was a new and improved version and Bob had asked if I would like to be the pilot for it.

This was a huge opportunity for me and I proceeded to find an owner of a Learjet who was open to modifying the aircraft to house the new Vectorvision system. After months of research and assisting Bob Nettmann in getting parts made for his new system, a new state-of-the-art camera system was born. I used to go to Bob's shop and actually run parts for him to get anodized and machined. I saw this as a great chance to do something wonderful as a movie film pilot and the hard work paid off as I eventually became one of less than a handful of pilots to do that type of flying.

I went on during my career, to have filmed 100's of airline commercials. I chased the Navy Blue Angels, USAF Thunderbirds, Canadian Snowbirds, filmed the highly secretive SR71, B-1 Bomber, B-2 Bomber, F-117, U2, X29, X31, and even NASA's Pegasus Rocket launch. I remember flying off the wing of a NASA B-52 as they launched a rocket from the wing of that huge plane while we filmed it. My journey has been nothing short of incredible and many flights of true adventure while getting paid at the same time.

I have had the honor of playing with clouds like a cat and mouse game, filming aircraft in flight around them, witnessing the most incredible sunsets, flying over the Barrier Reef in Australia at the crack of dawn, and flying through the mist of Victoria Falls and the snowcapped peak of Mt Kilimanjaro in Africa. I have witnessed the beauty of this earth that never ceases to amaze me. All the wonders here on this planet that God created, all the people who make an impact on our lives. Meeting and connecting with such people and observing such beauty has by far been one of the highlights of my career as a pilot and musician. It all has brought perspective to my life about what's important and what is not.

We all have our struggles, but in realizing our commonalities, those burdens become easier to shoulder. By recognizing that, the world becomes a more welcoming and optimistic place, allowing us to be better people and appreciate being alive. I have led my life with compassion and the understanding that I will never know everything and I will always be learning something. In that knowledge is room for growth. When trusting the process, there is faith in the unknown, in the mysterious ways in which God moves. And, there's an indescribable beauty in that. I think God created this world we live in to enjoy and cherish and that we will never know everything. As humans, we tend to think we have it all figured out when we actually have very little figured out but the creator of the Universe gives us bits and pieces on a need-to-know basis. We tend to think we're so significant when we really aren't in the big plan of life.

Flying above the atmosphere, the problems of our lives appear smaller. You begin to appreciate things as they truly are, to see a world where solutions are possible. All the dreaded things in life, all those moments we may not look forward to; the mundanity also holds beauty if you stop to see it. If you can realize that, you begin to appreciate and look at others with the compassion they deserve. As humans we all seek similar things in life, whether it's human connection, love, purpose; we all want our needs met and understood. Attempting to bridge the gap and listen to the people we love makes our lives here meaningful. As we stand on this world we call Earth, we are traveling around the sun at over 60,000 mph it makes me feel pretty insignificant but also knowing God has a plan for all of us and we are to cherish the gift of each day.

We sometimes gravitate towards others, hoping that they can fulfill something that feels missing in our lives. However, we fulfill that need when we approach our relationships with unconditional love and a servant's heart. We begin to learn what it means to lead with faith, kindness, and forgiveness.

Jeff in the Wolfe Air Learjet 25 with Vectorvision camera system for aerial filming. You can see the turret out the bottom.

Jeff flying photo Learjet filming a NASA X-29

REFLECTION POINT

We're not good at everything but great at something. What is it you're great at?

CHAPTER 4

ONE LIFE

I HAVE ALWAYS had a saying that flying a helicopter is like flying a magic carpet. I have several thousand hours of flight time before I received my helicopter rating. The company I flew for at the time, Cine/Exec Aviation had Learjet's and also four helicopters. Every chance I got, I would go in the helicopter with the other pilots and was always in awe of those machines. Eventually I racked up enough hours to obtain my Rotorcraft rating and from then on never looked back. Once rated I would end up landing on top of skyscrapers dropping passengers off for a dinner, flying wedding proposals, landing on mountain tops, Super Bowl arenas, NASCAR events, parties and Channel 9 News in Los Angeles. Some days I would fly the jet and helicopter in the same day. Maybe take a customer to Aspen and come back, then that afternoon fly Channel 9 News in the helicopter.

It is my heartfelt belief that we live in a time of many great blessings, but so many people seem to not know how to see the good in the world. It's the question we hear, is the glass half empty or is it half full?

We are bombarded with messages that tell us how divided everyone is from each other, constant news of doom and gloom, based on things that may or may not be true. These negative words break our hearts in little ways every day, causing us to lose perspective and faith in ourselves and humanity.

Fear is one thing that can alter our lives in a big way. When I look around, I see fear in many people. When Covid hit the world, there was fear among everyone and rightfully so because nobody knew what was going to happen. Fear can be a liar and can be a scary thing but we have to learn to overcome fear. God tells us so hundreds of times in the Bible. In flying aircraft, I have often been asked, "Have you ever been scared while flying?"

I always answer that I wouldn't be human or safe if I didn't have fear at times. I think we should respect fear but I don't think we should live in constant fear like God instructs us. Aviation has inherent fear because there's risk involved but as a pilot, I mitigate the risk with proper planning. There are a lot of things in life we fear as life itself has risk. Every time we get in our cars, there is risk but we mitigate risk by maintaining our vehicles, obeying the traffic laws, staying alert and driving defensively.

It was a beautiful Southern California afternoon, I was driving home from Burbank Airport and got paged, yes that crazy pager. I pulled off the freeway and found a pay phone. It was my boss and he said to turn around that they had announce the verdict of the Rodney King trial and there was rioting breaking out in Los Angeles. After my pre-flight I loaded the news crew and flew toward Los Angeles. A direct line from Burbank takes us right over Universal Studios through a pass. I will never forget the feeling I had as I crested the hill and got a glimpse of the Los Angeles basin. It was literally on fire from the rioting that had spread throughout the city. Within several hours our once peaceful city had turned into a firestorm of arson fires set. The Los Angeles riots were a humbling time that tested my resolve dealing with fear. Flying over that huge city the entire week at night with thousands of people rioting, looting and many even killed, brought an uncomfortable feeling to me that I had to deal with. It felt like I was in a war zone.

Risk will never be eliminated from our lives and fear is something we must overcome always. God tells us to do so. This journey of life is finite and no one knows how long we have. God wants us to live life to the fullest and enjoy this beautiful gift we have here.

One of our most interesting jobs was flying the A-Star for Wolfe Air filming the Space X parachute tests in Daggett, CA. The test involved dropping a 20,000 pound payload out of the back of a C-130 and test the emergency parachute system for the Space X capsule. It was a sight to behold to witness the giant chutes opening as we flew next to it filming it all the way to the ground. I would land on the dry lake bed and listen to the engineers discuss the results of the test. Helicopter flying is nothing short of miraculous, landing on mountain tops, flying through the cliffs of Sedona, Grand Canyon and well as performing gender reveal events, wedding proposals and events.

Jeff in the H5 Helicopter over the Grand Canyon

Flying has always brought me perspective about life, what a gift each day is. The feeling of being alone in a jet like the Eclipse at night in the middle of nowhere or flying through a canyon surrounded by cliffs and trees. It brings a feeling of gratitude.

Through faith, we must strive to live without fear and enjoy each day we have like a beautiful flight through the sky. There's a poem about two dates, the day we're born and the day we die with the dash in between. The dash is the sum total of this journey here and what we do while we are here. Only God knows the last date but the dash in between is what counts, what we did while we were here, how we treated people, the way we lived. Who did we affect? What kind of life did we lead? What did we do in our time here and how much kindness did we give out while we were here? We must not let fear consume us and let it run our lives. Fear is an enemy we must fight at all times. It's what inspired my song, *One Life*.

> I've got One Life I've been given One Life I've been living
> One life puts a smile on your face
> I've got One Life that's been forgiven One Life can make
> a difference All it takes is One Life
> To make this world a better place

Things begin to change when you focus on how you can effect a positive change, expanding in gratitude and having a servant's heart. Practicing the principles of a servant's heart will allow you to see what matters and give you the ability to create the life you want to live. If each person on the planet could do one act of kindness each day, we would transform the world overnight. Each day is a gift from God. What would happen if we acted like it?

Hopefully we first learn to serve at home from our parents, then use those skills in our relationships, friendships, families and workplace environments. Our childhood is kind of a pre-cursor to life and however we are brought up can dramatically impact the flight path of our lives. As we become adults, we get to practice and implement what we learned growing up in our marriages raising our children. Service starts at home, expands to our communities, then our country and ultimately the world. Then it ultimately ends up back at home every night.

A servant's heart in marriage, family and friendship is not about subservience. It asks, "What can I do for this person? How can I make their life better?" I want to make my spouse's life better because I love her. Hopefully she feels the same way and ultimately if that's the case it will be a marriage with that will thrive and succeed. If the relationship is based solely on "What's in it for me?" then what happens when the first-speed bump comes along? The relationship isn't sustainable. When you cannot see the other person's needs before yourself, that is ego, not love and the relationship is most likely to fail. The same applies to our loved ones, friends, and relationships. The world is a better place if we strive to have a servant's heart.

For those of us that end up in a marriage, there are vows that say "for better or worse". It is the ultimate commitment we make as humans and through thick or thin we bow to stay with that individual. A servant's heart has a better chance of weathering all the ups and downs. This holds true for all relationships: marriage, parenting, work, and friendships. Children, especially, benefit from seeing the servant's heart in action. I learned, after having children, that you kind of have to practice what you preach because they are smart. They are constantly watching to see if we practice what we preach. Children will watch their parents and the respect comes from when they see their mom or dad do what they say. It can't be a "do-as-I-say-not-as-I-do" mentality.

I was born in the beautiful city of Portland, Oregon. My mom, Daisy, was originally Canadian and a violinist and pianist in school. She played on the radio and even acted in a feature film with Cary Grant called *Sylvia Scarlett*. My Mom was raised very poor. They didn't have much but were taught the value of hard work.

As a little girl, her parents moved to Hollywood in search of a better life. My grandfather Henry was a gardener in Hollywood for many movie stars of the time. His wife: my grandmother, Violet, was from England and was a musician, violinist, and pianist. As a young girl, my mom was a red-headed child with a talent for music and acting. Living in Hollywood, she went to school with many kids of movie-star parents.

I used to love her stories. Once she told me about a friend that she had in high school named Mimi, who used to complain about her brother learning to play the trumpet. When she would visit her friend, the trumpet-playing would bother them. The young man would play and play until it drove my mom and her friend crazy.

Little did they know that the young trumpet player would one day become famous as an award-winning recording artist, Herb Albert. In another one of her stories, she told me how she had found a lost dog and put out a sign out in the neighborhood to help find the owner. One day they got a knock can on the door, and when they answered it, standing in front of them was the infamous Lucille Ball, completely thrilled to get her dog back.

Mom graduated from Fairfax High School in Hollywood and never went to college. She later met my biological dad, Robin, and after a courtship, got married. Shortly after that, I was born. When I was around three years old, they divorced, and my mom later remarried to Daniel Senour. He would adopt me and be the Dad I would grow up knowing, Dad Dan. My adopted father would teach me that I could capture my dreams.

When I was a young boy, I wanted a bicycle. He told me that he would pay for a portion of it, but I needed to come up with half first. It was my choice on how I made money, so I ended up mowing many lawns around my neighborhood. At the end of a few weeks, I had my money and, shortly afterward, I had my first bike.

Ever since I can remember I was taught that God created us to be productive. I was raised with the belief that hard work brings accomplishment and satisfaction to your life. God created us to work and be productive but then give back with a servant's heart.

My dad loved flying and was a private pilot. From as young as I can remember, I was strapped in the front seat of a Piper Cub while we took flight. I remember from a young age feeling the freedom of flight. It allowed me to see the world from such a different perspective. As we would fly along at 60 mph, Dad would open the side window of the Cub, and we would fly along with the earth below and the window open just like a bird. He served in the Air Force and ended up as a radar technician and engineer. When he was stationed in Alaska, it wasn't his first choice. But he was amazed by the pristine and wild beauty of Alaska.

His Mom and Dad, my grandma and grandpa Senour, grew up in Indiana. Grandma's dad, my great-grandpa, had a farm. One day she told me a story as a matter-of-fact about how her dad had a friend that flew airplanes, and on occasion, would fly in and land on their farm. She said that "Charlie" later became pretty famous as he flew across the ocean. I remember saying, "Grandma are you talking about Charles Lindbergh?" She answered with a confident "Yes." She told me that story long after I was a professional pilot, but I never got over how incredible my great grandfather was friends with Charles Lindbergh.

As I learned the way of a servant's heart in my youth, I now extend that compassion through my relationships, music, and piloting. On the surface, it may not seem like one person can impact the world. But I know that each voice and perspective can affect positive change. Everyone can lead with a servant's heart; it starts with how we treat ourselves, our families, and our neighbors. How do we embrace openness in a world more concerned with taking? We must be committed to the possibility and practice of unconditional love.

As a child, my dreams had no boundaries. I could see a future of optimism and abundance. I knew up in that Piper Cub as a boy marveling at the sight of the earth below that love could exist without limitations. Regardless of the hardship and turbulence that awaits us, the storms and bad weather that can confront us the greatest reward in life is to simply live and to not be afraid. Ultimately, we are in God's hands and he is the Captain of our ship. Beauty is always present, even along the sometimes dangerous and unexpected path before us.

CTS next to the H5 Sabercat helicopter

Jeff with H5 A-Star landing in a wedding reception

REFLECTION POINT

Things begin to change when you focus on expanding in gratitude and what will increase in your life. Make a gratitude list—write for 10 minutes without stopping and see how many blessings you can come up with.

CHAPTER 5

LONG WAY TO GO

IT DOESN'T MATTER where you start in life; what matters is that you keep going until you end up where you want to be. In Aviation we always have to have a destination. The only way we know how to be prepared to have a safe flight is to have a destination. By knowing where we're going we then can do a correct preflight, plan for the amount of fuel we need, make sure the weather is suitable to even go where we want to go.

In life there are only two destinations. God tells us in the Bible that we have the free will to choose our destination. It's either Heaven or Hell. The ticket to Heaven is very easy and spelled out by God. In John 3:16 "For God so loved the world, that he gave his only Son, that whoever believes in him shall have Eternal life. Eternity is a long time and to me an amazing destination to have in life.

Looking at the world 7 miles up from the lofty place of a cockpit taught me that finding joy in the simple things of life is the secret to happiness. When you see a city of 15 million people lit up below you on a moonlit night it brings perspective your mindset. I often look down at the population below and think of what's going on in all the lives at that very moment. If you could freeze time at any second during a day, there is every human emotion going on at once as I gaze at the huge city below.

Millions of lives happening all at once. I think about all the lives that are experiencing every feeling, every experience, every emotion humanly possible while I sit in my comfortable cockpit from thousands of feet up. It's humbling and thought-provoking and has taught me to love and appreciate the things I have in front of me, those simple things whether it is a hug from your child, a hot meal, running water, food, loved ones and the memories we acquire through this complex journey of life. It's taught me how precious each day is and the gift of life God has given each of us. These are the moments that have taught me about where the servant's heart begins.

Embracing the gifts God gave me has allowed me the ability to have a life I could never have imagined. But you cannot embrace what you are not grateful for. We seem to be surrounded by a world of envy rather than joy for others. Instead of focusing on what we don't have, I have tried to cherish what I do have and not be jealous or envious of others that have obtained success. I have had the opportunity to fly some of the wealthiest, most famous people on the planet around and not once have I ever felt envious. Actually, I have felt joy for them that they got to live and experience the American dream through their hard work. No matter how much I have there will always be someone with more as well as someone with far less.

No matter what we think is a liability, what we might classify as an obstacle, can become the thing that turns our lives into a beautiful story. I realize no matter how bad we might feel we have it, there is always somebody else that has it worse.

I remember my early 20s when I lived with a roommate in Van Nuys, pursuing my dream of becoming a pilot. I would work until I had saved enough to pay for an hour of flight instruction. Of course, I barely had the gas to drive to the field for my lesson, but it was all worth it for every second I got to spend in the air. We were two bachelors who could barely afford to pay our rent and even sometimes couldn't keep the gas turned on. On one occasion we couldn't afford our gas bill so they shut it off. We never once thought about asking anyone for help or the government for assistance. We just accepted in and told ourselves it would get better. For a month we learned how to deal with freezing showers and long winter nights with no heat. At least in Southern California it didn't snow. We did manage to find the money on occasion to buy music from time to time and would spend our evenings listening to records and figuring out the chords on our guitars. My roommate Cary and I would spend hours at Tower Records in Hollywood checking out which album we would purchase to head home and listen for hours. We ate instant ramen noodles most nights and sometimes splurged on hamburger helper after digging up some extra change to cover the bill at the grocery store. Those times gave us a foundation to turn our situations into better ones. My roommate went on to become a prominent architect and helped to design Universal Studios among other amazing places. I ended up as a career aviator, making a living at flying jets and helicopters. To this day, after over 30,000 hours logged, I still never tire of it and never take it for granted.

Those cold nights may seem distressing to most people, maybe even like a form of hardship. Yet, I would not trade anything in the world for them. The simple pleasures of music and food helped me to enjoy that chapter of my life and to appreciate what I did have, to live through it. While simple pleasures did not solve my problems, they eased the stress on my body and spirit. It was my faith in God quite honestly that always kept me going realizing that smooth skies lay ahead in my journey. Small graces can do that.

Embracing what you have, regardless of how it reflects your ideal, creates happiness where you are. It allows for a path where you can meet joy halfway, and as you do so, you begin to dream and see a future. Every part of your life leads you to where you are.

Regrets, adversity? They have formed the person you are today and inspired you to become better.

My parents always told me that anything good in life worth achieving takes lots of hard work, dedication, and faith in yourself. My dad's career in the tech industry meant he had to travel and move a lot for work. When I was a senior in high school, my dad transferred to Texas from our home in Southern California. I told my parents I didn't want to move again. Instead, I stayed in California with my best friend and his family. Even though I missed my family, I became independent at a young age.

After high school, I stayed in Southern California for college. I met a friend, Royce Jones, in college who was a flight instructor. I remember telling him I always wanted to learn to fly but couldn't afford it so I didn't know if or when I'd ever get to fly airplanes. I have been fortunate to meet people along the way that were willing to help, I met people who had a servant's heart and were willing to help me out, people that were mentors, giving of their time and resources. He said he would be willing to teach me if I paid for the airplane rental, besides he just wanted to go flying as well and what better way than to teach me at the same time. It was a win-win for both of us. So off we went on all kinds of adventures flying and all the while building my hours toward my license. I worked numerous jobs to cover my tuition and bills, then saved diligently to pay for the airplane rental. I learned to fly one hour at a time; that was all I could afford. Slowly, I obtained enough hours to get my pilot license and realized I wanted to pursue flying as a career.

It would be safe to say I worked about every conceivable job out there to finance my education and my flying ratings. Student loans didn't really exist then and my mom and dad weren't super wealthy. They helped but I had to figure out how to pay for the rest. From fast food to tutoring, jewelry shops, house cleaning, yard work, hanger sweeping, aircraft waxing, babysitting, inspecting printed circuit boards on an assembly line, even heavy construction, and driving a water truck during the summer. All of those jobs funded my flying habit and taught me that hard work opens doors. Mom used to tell me all the time "No matter what position you do, no matter how menial, always do it to the best of your ability."

So, I spent much of my time studying, learning to fly, and working. I didn't have a lot left over for a social life, but somehow, I still managed to have fun from time to time. I couldn't afford to fly much, so I'd round up my friends to pitch in on the cost of the airplane. Slowly but surely, I obtained my Private Pilot, Instrument, Commercial and Multi-Engine ratings and eventually the Doctorate of Aviation the Airline Transport Pilot rating. One of the biggest steps was when I obtained my Flight Instructor rating. Once I earned my Flight Instructor rating, I could start getting paid to do something I loved so much. I was in heaven. I loved to do flight instructing. The joy it gave me watching my students learn to fly an airplane and get hooked on the taste of freedom was priceless.

Some of my most nervous moments were when I would taxi to the side of the runway and get out to let my student do their first solo flight. I knew they were ready but never took for granted the responsibility of sending someone alone in the plane.

After instructing for about three years, I saved up enough money to obtain my Learjet type rating. I figured I might have a shot at a pilot job if I got my rating. A company at the Van Nuys airport had a Lear charter service. I visited them almost daily to politely let them know I was interested in flying with them. After much persistence, they called and asked if I was available the next day. My first jet job!

As a green co-pilot in a subsonic Learjet, there I was, off to Canada to drop off a customer then return home. I was in awe of the speed and climb rate of the small jet. It was like being in a rocket. It was challenging to keep my mind up to speed with the aircraft. After many hours, I finally got the hang of riding the jet-powered steed through the endless skies. There was so much to learn, but I was an eager apprentice. I flew with very experienced captains and learned to fly a marvel of aviation, the Learjet expertly. It's a challenging, unforgiving airplane to fly and takes a while to master. I relished every minute of the learning process.

My dream was to be a combat fighter pilot in the military and fly the fastest jet aircraft in the world. The thrill of pulling G's in a highly maneuverable aircraft and at the same time have the honor of serving my country. I longed to be in the cockpit. Sometimes, however, dreams are squashed before they even get started. When I was in my second year of college, I went to the Air Force and Navy recruiter to see what I had to do to fly fighter jets. When asked if I had perfect vision, I let them know I wore contact lenses. I was told in no uncertain terms that I had to have perfect vision to fly in the military and there were no exceptions. Today that requirement has changed but it didn't help me then. I was told that I could be a navigator in the back seat and I said that I had no interest in that. It devastated me and life had dished out a roadblock, a storm I had to overcome.

At that moment I could have chosen to give up on my dreams, and it would have been easy. Instead, I decided to embrace my ambitions and dreams and knew that if I didn't give up, I could achieve my goals so I decided to learn to fly as a civilian. I knew with hard enough work and dedication I could somehow, someway get my pilot ratings and eventually fly for a living. Who would have known that one day I would be the aerial chase pilot to film military demonstration teams like the Blue Angels, Thunderbirds and Canadian Snowbirds as well as many commercials and feature films. To this day, I still am in disbelief of the path God put me on and the blessed life of flying aircraft for a living.

Gratitude also makes it easier for you to reach your next level of life. In the American Constitution, the founding fathers promised us life, liberty, and the pursuit of happiness. It didn't guarantee happiness but the pursuit of it. You must work to obtain what will make you happy, but it seems like people have forgotten. Instead of being grateful for the opportunities they have been given, they look for all the things they do not have. Focusing on what is denied instead of what you have been given creates a prison for yourself of self-pity and greed.

One year we were contracted to film, believe it or not, a Japanese cigarette commercial, however they wanted to film it in Africa. It was for a brand called *Mild 7* Cigarettes. As we prepared to ferry the small jet halfway around the world, it took very intense flight planning to get it there. The Learjet 25 didn't have a long range, about 1,200 miles so we had to figure out how to get to Africa without running out of gas. From Burbank, we left flying with fuel stops in Nebraska, New York and St Johns, Newfoundland. Then on to the Azore Islands, Maiorca-Spain, Palermo-Italy, Cairo-Egypt, Djibouti at the Southern tip of the Red Sea and on to Nairobi-Kenya. Fuel stop after fuel stop, customs after customs, we eventually made it to our destination to meet our client.

Flying in Africa was an experience of a lifetime. There were no real rules like in the USA, not much radar coverage and witnessing cities along the way of 3rd world countries that were eye opening.

On our way there I remember flying over Ethiopia at night on our way to Nairobi. At the time there was a Civil War going on in Ethiopia and I remember thinking of the contrast between me in my tiny cockpit at 45,000 feet while flying over a war zone. It gave me perspective and made me realize how blessed we are in America as I saw how much of the world lived in situations that are difficult for us to imagine.

There was a study done by Boeing and they estimated that 80% of the world's population of 7.5 billion people had never stepped foot in an airplane. Pretty amazing to think about that. When we got to Nairobi, it was an eye opener. I had never seen people starving in the streets, women carrying jugs of water on their heads and just sheer poverty everywhere you turned. Yet they all seemed happy and content. The scenery of Africa was stunning as we filmed Mt. Kilimanjaro, Victoria Falls and endless tundra low-level filled with giraffes and flamingos. We filmed the top of Mt. Kilimanjaro, flew through the mist of Victoria Falls and observed wildlife from the air that was something out of a National Geographic magazine. It was like going back in time 500 years in many ways. My trip to Africa taught me a lot about gratitude and how blessed I really was. I often ponder the idea of how blessed I am to have been born in America as opposed to some third world country surrounded by poverty. I think every young person should have the opportunity to travel the world as it gives a whole new perspective on life.

One of my most challenging times flying and filming was while working on the movie *True Lies*. Meeting and working with Arnold Schwarzenegger and James Cameron was an honor.

I admired Arnold Schwarzenegger as he always seemed humble and kind. He came from nothing, was born in Austria, and later arrived in America. Arnold faced challenging circumstances in Austria, but he always approached his passions with resolution and focus. I had flown Arnold and his wife Maria Shriver on several occasions but never had any idea I eventually would be the aerial pilot on *True Lies*.

It was 1993 and I had just been hired as a pilot for Southwest but was asked to be the aerial pilot on *True Lies*. Fortunately, Southwest was very gracious in allowing me to film a SAG movie and was honored to get to work as a pilot for the well-known director James Cameron. I also got to be on the set of *True Lies*.

During the making of the movie, there was a five-acre piece of property in the Florida Keys with all the trucks and sets needed for the actors and crew. It included the catering truck and even a life-size mockup of a Harrier Jet. One of the funniest stories I have from the set was that I walked by and noticed this big semi-truck trailer with a gym in it one day. I went and asked this guy about it and if I could use it to get our workout in, and he said, "No, no, that's Arnold's gym. It's his gym that travels with him to the locations where Arnold shoots films so that he can still work out." I thought, *How cool is that!*

On occasion, they'd have tours of kids from different schools visiting to see the set. I noticed that Arnold was always gracious when signing autographs, joking around, and having fun with the kids. I thought that was one of his best qualities. It demonstrated that while he has faced hardship, he has succeeded despite the odds but worked hard. His ability to truly see and relate to others is a sign of a servant's heart. Gratitude, or joy in what you have, is how you are free to serve others with love. If you cannot appreciate what you have, right here and now, you do not give your time and possessions freely.

When you look back at the beginning of his career and his first movies, he had minor acting roles, maybe saying only two words. His acting skills only got better over time. He's an example of the classic rags to riches story, living the American dream. People who come from nothing are often very grateful when they succeed.

Working on *True Lies* was one of the most challenging flying jobs I ever had though. The scene we especially difficult to prepare for as they wanted me to film the Harrier Jet doing a strafing run on the bridge. James Cameron actually purchased part of the old section of bridge in the Florida Keys to do the scene. The scene had to be executed and timed perfectly to make it usable. Charges were set in the water and angled to the bridge. The truck was moving at 50 mph and we were moving at 300 mph. We had to line up the flight path of the Harrier Jet with our Learjet to film as well as the charges in the water and the truck on the bridge. Any part of it not timed right or lined up correctly would result in an unusable shot. As I briefed the flight with James Cameron, the producer, I told him I needed some time to rehearse the shot to set up the timing. He responded by telling me that I could rehearse all I wanted but when I thought I was ready, it had better work. I said, "Yes sir."

Tucked over the shoulder in formation with the Harrier Jet, I talked the pilot into position as I would instruct him by radio to come left, come right, drop down slightly, adjust. Then I would tell the truck driver on the bridge to start and hopefully the timing would work out. It took about 5 dry run rehearsals to figure out the timing and I finally told Mr. Cameron that we were ready. As we set up for the shot, I was nervous but confident. I will never forget the sight of the charges in the water going off like a machine gun strafing run from the Harrier Jet, the truck on the bridge getting blown up as we passed overhead. It was a success and we celebrated but not without tension.

Life is like that, we have to rehearse, prepare and execute a plan that sometimes we're nervous and don't know the outcome but if we don't try will never know what would have been.

In the Bible, gratitude is vital for living a good life. 1 Thessalonians 5:18 (New Revised Standard Version) says, "Give thanks in all circumstances; for this is the will of God in Christ Jesus for you." In all of our struggles and joys, there are opportunities for us to grow in understanding what it means to love ourselves and each other genuinely.

Philippians 4:11–13 (English Standard Version) states it best: "Not that I am speaking of being in need, for I have learned in whatever situation I am to be content. I know how to be brought low, and I know how to abound. In any and every circumstance, I have learned the secret of facing plenty and hunger, abundance and need. I can do all things through him who strengthens me."

Gratitude is the key to enjoying the journey. Life isn't painless, but with gratitude, there is contentment. Through contentment, we learn to live a better life, to know ourselves when we either have nothing or overflow with abundance. We can then know others and love them; because we have learned it first within ourselves and our relationship with God.

CTS on Main Stage at Soulfest

CTS performing at Dream City Church, Phoenix

REFLECTION POINT

It doesn't matter where you start in life; what matters is that you keep going until you end up where you want to be. Where is it you want to be?

CHAPTER 6

TOO GOOD TO BE REAL

GRATITUDE ALLOWS YOU to see beyond the pain of your current circumstances and allows you to be ready to see the next steps that God has in store for you.

If I had focused on the hurts of my heart, I might have missed the best and most perfect gift that was hand-delivered to me. It is not often that you can say that love has knocked on your front door.

After my divorce, I moved into a tiny apartment as a temporary place until I found a home to purchase. The apartment actually had some wonderful memories as I spent time with my kids and we had a lot of fun. It was cramped though so I was excited to find a home. I eventually bought a house in a beautiful rural neighborhood near Phoenix. Once we moved in it was the start of a beautiful new chapter. There was plenty of room for my kids, a great neighborhood and I decided to put in a pool. After about 3 weeks had passed, there was a knock on the door one day. I had my youngest Son, Parker with me at the time. He was around 4 years old.

As I opened the door, there stood a beautiful Woman. From the moment I laid eyes on her I knew there was something very special about her. I didn't know what but it was a feeling I had.

I asked who she was and she said, "My name is Allison. I'm the person you bought your house from. I happened to be in the neighborhood visiting some friends and thought I'd stop by to see how you liked the house and if everything was alright with your move in."

Parker reached out his hand and said, "Hi I'm Parker, it's nice to meet you."

I invited her in and we talked for awhile. Little did I now but God had just place a miracle in my life as he placed the love of my life on my front doorstep. We talked for a while and something told me to get her number. Following that intuition led to a beautiful and life-giving relationship that has blessed me and my children. Allison has become one of my life's greatest joys and I have a divorce to thank for bringing us together. Hardship can be a silver lining, and uncertainty is the promise for a new day. Gratitude allows you to see beyond the pain of your current circumstances and be ready for what God has in store for you. If I had focused on the hurt the heartbreak, I might have missed this opportunity for love. I will always be grateful and aware of the circumstances that led me to Allison.

When I married Allison, I shared custody of my children with my ex wife. Things can change in life though, like a storm in our path or an emergency that pops up. Little did I know I would end up with the kids full time and Allison would end up being a pivotal role in raising them. We were a package deal. Compromise, compassion, and thankfulness are the signs of a servant's heart. Allison is with me on my mission and my one life, by God's grace. It was only 3 weeks after meeting Allison that I wrote the song, "Too Good To Be Real

She went from being a flight attendant to traveling the world and scuba diving in places most people haven't even heard of to the life of a servent's heart in charge of kid's schedules, events, activities and being an integral part of her new family. It is not an easy adjustment to make from being a master of your own time to being at the service of four children. But there is also a joy that comes with making this choice. We have created a family life that is beautiful and will give our children the jumping board to create their own families. Life does not always go the way we want. There is an old saying that says "Man plans and God laughs." It is not that he enjoys watching us be uncomfortable. Rather, he understands that we want it all to be easy, but easy will never teach us what we really need to learn to move forward into the best version of yourself. That is why focus is so important.

"For where your treasure is, there your heart will be also."

—Matthew 6:21.

Treasure is more than just gold, jewels, and luxury cars. It is something far more valuable. It is where your time goes, whether it is helping your kids with homework, listening to music, or spending quality time with those you love. This entire journey of life no matter how rich or famous we are really comes down to the memories we make with our loved ones and the legacies we leave behind. I once heard a saying that there's no U-Haul behind a Hearst. All of our worldly belongings are really just on loan for awhile as we navigate through this life.

What are you focusing on at this moment? Is it the things you do not like or is it on the things that are good? Servanthood is more than just action. It is also a state of mind, where you decide to create the best places for you, the people you love, and the communities you serve. Focus is an essential part of the servant's heart. It allows you to see where you can be of service and maintain that service.

If you find yourself in a situation that is not what you planned it to be, you have the choice to focus on the good or bad. To choose to focus on the good does not mean that you are ignoring the bad parts and avoiding consequences. It means that you are aware that there is a better thing happening that goes above the anger, sadness, bitterness, or fears that you may be experiencing. The Bible is very clear that what we focus on will determine our path. If all you can see is bad in the world because that is all you choose to see, then life will be much harder for you.

It is not easy when we are bombarded with videos, images, and stories of people suffering, families divided, and countries at war every day. I am not saying to cut off all current events. We are called to be salt and light in the world, and we cannot do that if we are unaware of what needs healing and help. However, Philippians 4:8 offers a solution: "Finally, brothers, whatever is true, whatever is honorable, whatever is just, whatever is pure, whatever is lovely, whatever is commendable, if there is any excellence, if there is anything worthy of praise, think about these things."

Changing your focus is one of the most powerful things you can do to decide who you are going to be. When I was told that I could not join the Air Force, I did not let it hold me back. Instead, I focused on the actions I could take. I could study to become a civilian pilot. So, I did. Then I learned how to fly jets, so I could fly stunt plans for military movies and shows. Then I learned how to fly passenger airplanes for a 20-year career with Southwest. Every step was because I chose to focus on what was good in my life and what actions I could take to support that good. With those actions, I was able to be a better husband, father, and friend.

Jeff on the Southwest Boeing waving to the passengers in the terminal

When we think about the direction of our lives, safety and honoring what we need are essential to our well-being. As everyone is given one life, we must protect ourselves and practice a servant's heart out there in the world. When it comes to airplanes, one of the most important parts is a magnetic compass which points to the magnetic north. Magnetic north is not the same as true north (where the North Star is), in fact, there's a 13-degree difference. Without that compass, pilots would be unable to know where we're going, the direction we are headed, and we won't end up in the right city or destination. Every time we takeoff in an aircraft we have to know our destination, where are we going? Otherwise we have no idea how to prepare for that flight, how much fuel to take, is the weather suitable for landing. In life we have to always consider what's our destination? What's the real purpose of this journey, where are we going and how do we get there?

Life is similar, having a moral and directional compass is life-saving. How we treat and interact with people out there in the world reflects our values and ourselves. Having a sense of drive and focus guides us to do things of our own free will. In my life, God is my compass, he plants my feet on the ground and guides me in the right direction. He created each of us with talents and gifts, and with our own ability to make a change.

Once I flew someone to Aspen, a wealthy Individual who wasn't very famous. The weather in Aspen became a bit troublesome, and safety is always my priority as a pilot, so I told him that we couldn't get into Aspen safely. I said, "We have to go to Grand Junction or Denver."

He replied eagerly, "No, I have to go to Aspen." "We can't. The weather's down."

Aspen is one of the most challenging airports in the country to get in and out of. The deep valley is surrounded by mountains, it's also very tentative, and when the weather is bad, it's even worse.

He kept insisting.

So, I said, "Ok, here's the deal. It's either Denver or Grand Junction. So, you let me know and we'll go there."

Finally, he agreed, "Okay, okay, Denver. Let's go to Denver."

As a pilot, I know that you should never feel pressured to make a bad choice that compromises safety, regardless of if someone is rich or famous. That was a time when my moral compass guided me to do the right thing.

Gratitude also gives perspective about yourself in the world. I did a film job in Africa flying a jet once for that Japanese cigarette commercial. One of the shots they wanted to obtain was Mount Kilimanjaro, which is, around 18,000 feet high. Ideally, we would have gotten a helicopter shot with a camera mount on it, but it's too high for a helicopter. So, instead, we used our Learjet, briefed it and we would do these low, slow passes, right by the peak of Mount Kilimanjaro. At the top of it there is this kind of crater-looking thing with this glacial blue ice type of pool of water out there, it's just beautiful. We ferried the plane across the world to go to Africa and the airplane didn't have a long fuel range like airliners do. So, we loaded up the camera system and the crew and flew to Africa.

We went through St. John's, Newfoundland, we then across to the islands in Majorca, Spain, and, and then down to Cairo, Egypt. And then from Cairo, we went to Djibouti, which is at the south edge of the Red Sea, basically stopping in Djibouti for fuel.

Cairo was also stunning. You're flying over the pyramids and all these ancient sites that are marvels of human capability and spirit. As we were flying over the pyramids, Djibouti from earlier was kind of stuck in my mind. We landed, and shut the engines down, and I got up and opened the door. When flying in all these different countries you are greeted by their security, and customs people.

Then, you got to show your paperwork and your passport so they can verify you. When I get out there are five people, around 19–20 years old surrounding the plane, each of them with a machine gun. 1000s of things go through your mind at that moment. What the heck am I getting myself into here? Of course, you abide by their rules and their customs. It ended up being fine, and we were safe. It was just strange to see these kids who were not old enough to drive caught in a war zone.

Djibouti was extremely humid and at the southern edge of the Red Sea. We went from Djibouti to Nairobi, and it was at night. At the time, we had to overfly Ethiopia to get to Nairobi, which is in Kenya. And at the time, there was a civil war going on in Ethiopia. And in the irony to me of being in a jet at 45,000 feet over Ethiopia at night, in his comfortable capsule of a jet going 600 miles an hour, and you look down on the ground, it's very dark. That's a difference between flying over the US versus Africa; in the US there are lights everywhere below as you pilot. Across Africa, there is pitch darkness, there are no roads, lights, or cities. I remember looking down into the darkness of the night and thinking *we're over Ethiopia and there are people being killed down there below us. There's a war going on. We flew right over it.* And it was just the weirdest, most heartbreaking feeling. We were so protected in this little capsule.

In Nairobi (which is a big city) when filming the commercial we stayed in a nice hotel. The producers of the commercial had a picture of

Mount Kilimanjaro, which was from a magazine. It was this beautiful glacial blue ice that was taken in the middle of winter. The producers described it as a donut. Every day we'd fly the plane over Kilimanjaro and shoot footage. They said it didn't resemble the donut in the picture because there was no snow glazed over the top of the mountain. But they still wanted to go every day and witness their "ice donut" for themselves.

So, finally, I told him, "Look, there's not going to be a donut until there's a storm, it's fruitless for us to go up here every day."

I talked them into leaving the footage as it was for the commercial, and not searching for this ice donut. They then decided they wanted footage of Victoria Falls. So, we ferried the plane down to where Victoria Falls was. Zimbabwe and three countries surround Victoria Falls. There's the Zambezi River, a huge river, like the Mississippi. It's similar to Niagara Falls in a way, absolutely gorgeous. In places like Africa, flying-wise, pretty much anything goes; it's not as regulated. The producers wanted to go pretty low, near the mist, because the river flows out and falls beautifully.

There's a cloudy mist from the falls, and they wanted me to go right through and film it. While they didn't get the donut footage they wanted, we did produce amazing results for the commercial.

The irony of that flight over Victoria Falls was that as I shot footage, there were people on one side of the resort hotel, who were out by the pool, admiring this gorgeous location. But as we'd fly, we'd go across the falls into the neighboring countries. On the other side of this border were natives with huts, spears, carrying water from miles away. It was just such an incredible and almost shocking contrast.

In Africa, I witnessed people who didn't have running water. Women would walk down the street with a big jug of water on their heads, probably having hiked miles just to get fresh water. Seeing how people live all over the world has given me a sense of gratitude for what I do have. I wish it was a requirement for everyone to travel and see how others live. I think it opens people's minds and hearts to the reality of experiences outside their own. Not everything or everyone looks and is like you. We must share gratitude for our similarities and differences as people.

A servant's heart is not just about your own needs and wants, you must serve your communities and world. Every day I wake up and thank God for the gift of another day. God helps me make this possible. Any day we get to be alive on this planet is a gift, one given to us. I don't want to take advantage of that, to ever lose sight of what a blessing it is to have this one life.

We get to be in charge of our choices as we navigate and find our North. God is there to guide us, reminding us of our purpose, free will, and all our blessings. We can lead with a servant's heart, become a light among the darkness, guiding others through this journey of life as we cultivate gratitude.

REFLECTION POINT

Gratitude allows you to see beyond the pain of your current circumstances and allows you to be ready to see the next steps that God has in store for you. What pain do you need to let go of in order to move forward?

CHAPTER 7

ANGEL WITH A BROKEN WING

AFTER FLYING HALFWAY across the world to the capital of Bulgaria, Sofia, we drove six hours across what looked like the Siberian tundra, a snow-covered barren landscape. The town was full of depressing gray rectangles and white snowdrifts, making it difficult to maintain our bearings in these pre-GPS times.

It was the year 2000 and we were looking for an orphanage. Our driver didn't know where its location was so we stopped to ask locals for some help. On the outskirts of town, there was a goat herder with his staff and sheep in traditional garb. I already felt like I was on some strange exodus but seeing a reminder of biblical times was not what I thought I would be seeing that day.

Thankfully, our driver spoke his dialect and he was able to direct us to the orphanage. As we drove, I thought about my newly adopted daughter, Silvia. She was waiting for us to pick her up and bring her to a forever home.

People in Bulgaria were just waking up from a communist regime with a newfound sense of freedom. They were welcoming democracy into their lives, starting to truly express themselves. Post-communist eastern Europe was in flux, forcing mothers to make difficult decisions, especially for mothers of people born like Silvia. She was born with a disabled arm and left at an orphanage. We do not know why or how it happened, but we do know that when we saw a picture of this beautiful baby girl, my wife and I were drawn to her. We went through the proper channels and started the adoption process.

I was swarmed by children of all sizes and abilities when I stepped through the door of the orphanage. There was so much need, but only so much that I could do that day. After saying goodbye to my new friends, we went to meet our daughter. Silvia was frightened of us and of leaving the orphanage. Yes, it was not the best environment, but she had no idea that she was being taken to a new home. In retrospect, I can see how I have fought God in similar circumstances. Through the ride to the airport, on the plane, and on the ride to our house, Silvia sat in a fetal position and sucked her thumb. She did not improve when she arrived home, refusing to eat up to the point where she required hospitalization.

Jeff with his Daughter Silvia whom was adopted from Bulgaria

We did not understand what was going on inside of her at the time, but the change was too much for her mind to process and she went into shock. Silvia stayed in the hospital for 10 days, being fed via IV. They put a feeding tube into her, running through her nose into her stomach so that we could take her home. Feeding her that way was still an ordeal, as she would choke on the food passing through.

When we imagined adopting a child, this was not what we had in mind. Love is not always easy, at least not the kind that changes lives. It requires a commitment to weather the good and the bad, and not being afraid to reach out to those around you.

Love is not a feeling, it's a way you live your life. Love is not something you give or take; it's something you make a choice each day to embody in your mind, heart, and actions.

Luke 10:25–37 is the story of the Good Samaritan. It is a familiar tale, but it means so much more when you understand the history behind it. Jewish religious law placed a priority on physical cleanliness. Being physically clean meant you were spiritually clean, but there were ways you could become and be considered unclean. You could not touch someone who was injured, even if it meant helping them. The Jewish man in the ditch was avoided by spiritual leaders because they were afraid for themselves and prioritized their standing over the wellbeing of this man. It was also unclean to touch someone who was not Jewish. It was known in society that, if you were not Jewish, you did not touch a Jewish person or their belongings. The Samaritan was not Jewish, and he chose to go against what society says is the right thing to do to help the man in the ditch. He chose loving others over the easy thing to do.

Silvia eventually got the hang of her new home and began eating on her own. She called me "Daddy" and grew into a bright, joyful young woman who is learning how to make a life for herself. There were developmental challenges and frustrations that came along with it. But if we had chosen the easy way, we would never have known the joy of our daughter, Silvia. When she walks into her job at the local grocery store, people treat her like a rock star, because of the kindness she shows to the shoppers and her coworkers. She chooses to love every day, and she is now an indispensable part of the community. Now 24, Silvia is a bright light who shines on the lives of others. She lives on her own and has a roommate, pays her own bills, and stays busy and productive. She has lived her whole life with just one hand, but she's never once complained about it.

My goal for her is that she finds love and her own sense of happiness. Our daughter lives a couple of miles from us, has a lot of friends and support, and is an essential part of our lives.

I wrote a song called *Angel with a Broken Wing*, which she inspired. It has a message behind it. We never treated her any differently or loved her differently than our other children. As she was growing up, there were even times when we forgot her limitations. While she doesn't have one hand, she has adapted masterfully. She is incredibly capable; she has tried prosthetics but didn't like them or none of them were comfortable enough. Silvia ties her shoes with one hand and rides a bicycle to work every day. When it rains, she Ubers to work, but she loves feeling independent. Everyone around town knows or has seen this little girl that is hardworking and who's really friendly with the customers at Albertsons. She's just a good, kind-hearted human being. Silvia has shown what it means to lead with a servant's heart and persevere in the face of hardship.

Making the choice to love when it's hard is the hallmark of the servant's heart. It might be the hardest part of choosing to serve others because it does not always come with a reward. Sometimes, it will be more difficult than you anticipated. But the payoff can be so much more than you ever dreamed. Consistent love resulted in the daughter we know today, who I wouldn't trade for the world.

Choosing love does not always look like an act of heroism. It is picking up your socks from the floor and putting them in the hamper because it makes it easier for your wife. It is cleaning up dog poop when your kids forgot to let Sparky out or holding your tongue when someone says something unfortunate about your favorite politician.

A servant's heart seeks to serve others, even when it is inconvenient or uncomfortable to be kind.

We are called to serve, but that service comes with a requirement to love others. Otherwise, our actions are no more than the "clanging cymbal," spoken of in 1 Corinthians 13. No matter what religion or philosophy you believe in, that passage gives the best directions for living in love. "If I speak in the tongues of men and of angels, but have not love, I am a noisy gong or a clanging cymbal. And if I have prophetic powers, and understand all mysteries and all knowledge, and if I have all faith, so as to remove mountains, but have not love, I am nothing. If I give away all I have, and if I deliver up my body to be burned, but have not love, I gain nothing. Love is patient and kind; love does not envy or boast; it is not arrogant or rude. It does not insist on its own way; it is not irritable or resentful; it does not rejoice at wrongdoing but rejoices with the truth." 1 Corinthians 13–16.

There are a lot of things in our world that would change if we chose to love before we opened our mouths. We would see fewer divisions and more people working together. Maybe the nightly news would be a little less stressful if we could decide to act in love more often.

While I've faced a lot of difficult situations in my life, I've always chosen the act of love when confronted with the seemingly impossible. To lead with a servant's heart has been simply doing what God has led me to do. I've had a life of lessons, some of them more painful and more challenging than others, but have always stayed true to myself and have kept my heart open.

I have piloted for film and TV, flown famous stars around the globe, traveled, and expressed myself through music. In addition to my career, I have nurtured a family and taught them the importance of God and serving their communities. Showing my family what it means to have a servant's heart has taught me to always keep an open mind and to know compassion and compromise. My adopted daughter Silvia has shown me how to love in a way that I hadn't known before, to love her as my own. My parents instilled in me a patient love, one which realizes the value of hard work.

I've realized so much of what I wanted to do and made reality so many other things I once didn't dare to dream. Life is rarely smooth or predictable, it's not unlike flying in that way. Flying is in my blood, it's as much a part of who I am as all the words and experiences that brought me here.

I think humans were meant to fly, so we created the resources and technology to make that happen. It was hundreds of years of dreaming and perfecting, some even risked their lives for the promise of flight. It took a lot of trial and error and demanded a lot of research and experimentation, but if humans have proven anything it's that we're optimistic. People are constantly searching for something bigger and brighter themselves, something that allows them to feel closer to the big picture.

Looking at the sky, whether you're on the ground or in the comfort of a cockpit, encourages us to imagine the life of what's around us. I'm still the boy that I was: excited by that possibility, looking up and seeing the limitless horizon. I have kept my heart open to the beauty this world has to offer.

Jeff flying the Wolfe Air Learjet filming a 787 for Boeing

Jeff's retirement flight on Southwest Airlines.
Two water cannon salute from the fire department.

REFLECTION POINT

Love is not a feeling, it's a way you live your life. What action can you take to choose to love today?

Album Cover "Angels Watching Over Me"
hit #16 on Global Radio Charts.

Jeff with Marine on stage at concert Mesa Performing
Arts Center along with High School orchestra

Jeff at Soulfest in Gunstock Ski Resort Massachusetts.
Candlelight service in front of 10,000 people.
The audience is on a ski slope.

Jeff with Alice Cooper holding Jeff's book

Jeff in Boeing Max Southwest jet with Southwest guitar given to him by Gary Kelly Southwest CEO

Jeff on stage in Texas for Snowball Express Goldstar families

Jeff receiving the President's Award from Southwest Airlines in 2015

Jeff on various stages

Band Photo- Left to Right- Jerry Nuzum,
Jeff Senour, Joe McGinnity, Dylan Elliott

Jeff going for first skydiving experience.
Never too old or too afraid to try something new

CTS inside a corporate jet.

www.ingramcontent.com/pod-product-compliance
Lightning Source LLC
Chambersburg PA
CBHW051548120626
46551CB00013B/1422